From Your Friends at The MAILBOX®

D1063108

COMPREHENSION CONNECTIONS

Build Comprehension Skills With Science & Social Studies Passages

Grade 3

Project Editor
Amy Erickson

Writers
Rebecca Brudwick, Julie Granchelli,
Erin Harp, Laura Wagner

Editors
Scott Lyons, Leanne Stratton

Art Coordinator
Donna K. Teal

Artists
Theresa Lewis Goode, Sheila Krill, Mary Lester, Greg D. Rieves,
Rebecca Saunders, Barry Slate, Donna K. Teal

Cover Artists
Nick Greenwood, Clevell Harris, Kimberly Richard

www.themailbox.com

©2001 by THE EDUCATION CENTER, INC.
All rights reserved.
ISBN #1-56234-427-7

Manufactured in the United States

10 9 8 7 6 5 4 3 2

TABLE OF CONTENTS

MAKING CONNECTIONS

What's the key to comprehension? Connections! Connections between words and meanings, between text and concepts, and between text and prior knowledge. Not only do these connections help students understand what they read, but they help them recall it, too!

Most students do not make these connections on their own, though. They need to be taught how. Learning a variety of strategies that they can use before, during, or after reading helps youngsters make these links and boosts comprehension.

> **Choose from among the tried-and-true strategies described here to match your students' needs. They're perfect for promoting comprehension of the passages in this book and of countless other reading materials!**

Before Reading

What do students already know about a topic? What misconceptions do they have? What experiences have they had with the concepts? The answers to these questions all relate to prior knowledge—the information and experiences that a student brings to a reading situation.

> Prior knowledge has a tremendous impact on comprehension because readers combine information from text with what they already know in order to gain meaning. Tap into prior knowledge and increase comprehension with the quick and easy ideas below.

- **It's in the Cards!:** Invite students to brainstorm words related to the reading topic. Write each word on a separate card. Ask students to group the cards and to explain their reasoning. If desired, post the grouped cards on a board. After youngsters read the text, have them revisit the groupings and make changes as appropriate to reflect the information they learned.

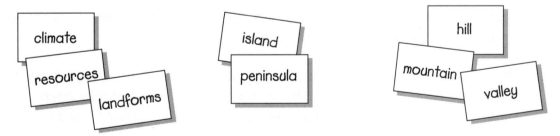

- **Set a Purpose:** Guide each youngster in setting a purpose for reading, such as finding the answer to a question or finding the most important sentence in a passage.

- **Take a Look!:** Encourage students to read the title and look at the illustrations. Then have them share their observations and predict what they will learn from the text.

During Reading

Does it make sense? This all-important question is one that good readers frequently ask themselves. In fact, they constantly self-monitor their reading. Use the following ideas to heighten students' awareness of their comprehension as they read.

- **Think-Alouds:** Model this strategy by sharing your thought processes as you read aloud, interrupting your reading to verbally insert your predictions, context clues that you use, things you're wondering about…in short, any thoughts you have about the text. As you resume your reading, model how you pick up the train of thought where you left off. After several demonstrations, have students try the strategy in small groups.

- **Partner Up!:** This idea works well for multiparagraph passages. Pair students. One student in each pair reads the first paragraph to his partner. The listener summarizes the paragraph. The partners switch roles and then continue reading and summarizing the rest of the passage.

- **Stop and Restate:** Encourage each student to read a passage in small sections, stopping after each section to silently restate what he has read. If he has trouble restating at any point, he rereads the relevant section.

After Reading

So what was the passage about? Do you agree with the author? Continue the reading process with questions like these to help students fully understand the text. Here are some other effective follow-ups:

- **Picture-Perfect:** As soon as students finish reading a passage, invite them to describe any pictures they made in their heads as they were reading.

- **In Search Of:** Ask students literal and inferential questions about the passage. Have them determine whether each answer is "right there" in the passage, whether they need to "read between the lines" to find it, or whether they need to use their own opinions and experiences to answer.

- **Graphic Organizers:** Have youngsters organize and process the information they learned from reading by having each one use a copy of a provided graphic organizer (see pages 60 and 61) or inviting them to make their own webs and charts. For a whole-class follow-up, make a transparency of a graphic organizer and complete it with students.

ABOUT THIS BOOK
Overview

It's no secret that time is a precious commodity for teachers. So why not maximize it (and student learning!) by reinforcing reading skills and content area concepts at the same time? This book will help you do exactly that. Each comprehension unit is based on common science or social studies standards. Because each unit is three pages long, students have multiple opportunities to read about the same topic or theme. This repeated exposure helps them build prior knowledge and further strengthens comprehension.

Most text lends itself to practice with a few different comprehension skills. The passages in this book are no exception. The most significant skills on each page are indicated at the top of it.

Before Students Start

The words below are used in student directions in this book. For best results, familiarize students with the words before assigning any pages that include them.

- ***Passage:*** Explain that a passage is a piece of writing—not a story.
- ***Thoughts*** and ***Ideas:*** Many of the questions in this book ask students to write their thoughts or ideas. Point out that there is no one right answer for any of these questions, but that students should be able to support their reasoning.
- ***Column:*** Tell students that one way to organize words is by placing them in labeled columns, grouped under the appropriate headings.

In Every Unit

- **Prior Knowledge Question:** A question above each passage helps you set the stage for students' reading.

- **Words to Know:** Critical vocabulary words are noted. To introduce a word, try one or more of these ideas:
  — Discuss any multiple meanings.
  — Help students use familiar word parts to determine the word and its meaning.
  — Demonstrate what the word means; show the item it names or a picture of it.
  — Have students predict the meaning and an appropriate use of the word by dictating a sentence for it. Ask them to read the passage to check their ideas and then revise the sentence if needed.

- **Passage:** Encourage students to read each passage more than once to increase fluency and, as a result, comprehension.

- **Brain Builder:** A question for each passage promotes reflection and higher-level thinking. Use it as part of the assignment rather than as a bonus in order to ensure that all students have rich, thought-provoking experiences with the text.

What do you know about
living things?

People, Animals, and Plants

Think about a baby, an elephant, and a
sunflower. They are all different, but they have
something in common. They are all alive. All
living things breathe, reproduce, and grow. They
all need energy.

People and some animals use lungs to
breathe. Fish use gills to take in oxygen.
Insects breathe through tiny holes in their bodies.
Plants take in oxygen through their leaves.

When some living things reproduce, they have
many offspring at once. Others have only one or
two. People have babies. Plants make seeds.
Birds and some other animals lay eggs. Energy
from food helps living things grow.

Big, small, plant, or animal, all living
things are alike in many ways!

Words to Know
reproduce
energy
oxygen

1. **Look** back in the passage. **List** three things that all living things do.

   _____

   _____

2. **Circle** the word in the passage that means "young living things."

3. **Underline** the sentence in the passage that tells why living things need energy.

4. **Think** about the passage. What is one way that fish and plants are alike? Different? _____

   _____

On the back of this sheet, list three living things that you have seen
during the last few days. Write how you know they are living.

Brain Builder

What might happen if an animal's habitat changes?

Giant Pandas in Danger

What happens when an animal's habitat changes? Giant pandas know. The pandas live in bamboo forests in China. Some forests have died or been cut. Now it is hard for pandas to find bamboo.

Bamboo is just about the only food that pandas eat. Pandas eat a lot of bamboo to get the energy they need. A panda might eat more than 40 pounds of bamboo a day!

There are not many pandas left. They are rare. Some people are trying to help them so that they do not become extinct. The people are putting land aside for the pandas. They are planting bamboo, too. Some scientists study pandas to learn more ways to protect them.

1. **Read** each word in the left column. **Find** its meaning in the right column. **Write** the correct letter in each blank.

    _____ habitat   a. not living any longer
    _____ extinct   b. home
    _____ rare   c. not seen very often

2. **Read** each sentence below. **Write** "F" for each fact. **Write** "O" for each opinion.

    a. _____ There are not many giant pandas left in China.
    b. _____ Pandas are the cutest mammals.
    c. _____ Everyone should try to help the pandas.

3. **Think** about the passage. Why do you think there are not many giant pandas?

    _____

Brain Builder

Look back at the title. Why do you think the author chose it? Write your ideas on the back of this sheet.

Name _____

Classification, drawing conclusions, main idea

How do living things get their food?

Green plants can do something that no other living things can do. They can use sunlight to make their own food! They use the energy from the sun to produce it. Trees, daisies, and other plants are producers.

Other living things, such as cows, cannot make their own food. Cows eat grass to get energy. The grass holds energy from the sun. The energy is passed to the cows. Cows, squirrels, and other animals that eat plants are consumers. Not all consumers eat plants. Some consumers depend on animals instead. Other consumers depend on both plants and animals. Raccoons eat bugs, fruit, and many other things, for example. Energy goes from one living thing to another.

Words to Know

producer   consumer

depend

1. **Read** the words below. **Write** "P" for each producer. **Write** "C" for each consumer.

   a. _____ apple tree   d. _____ grass

   b. _____ ladybug   e. _____ raccoon

   c. _____ cow   f. _____ daisy

2. **Think** about the passage. Why is the sun important to cows? _____
   _____

3. What is a good title for this passage? Why? _____
   _____

Brain Builder

Think about the passage. How do people depend on both plants and animals for energy? Write your ideas on the back of this sheet.

LIVING THINGS: *Producers & consumers*

What things does a plant need to be healthy?

Words to Know

enough

amount

wilt

Just Right!

A plant cannot talk, but it can let people know whether it is healthy. How a plant looks gives clues about whether it is getting the things it needs. All plants need air, light, and water to live. If they do not get these things in the right amounts, they will not grow well. Different plants need different amounts of light, shade, and water.

If plants do not get enough water, they will wilt, but if they get too much water, they will die. Plants that do not get plenty of light will turn yellow. Their stems might become long and thin.

People who take care of plants should observe them closely for signs of what they need!

1. **Look** back in the passage. **Circle** the word that means "watch."

2. How does a plant let you know whether it is healthy? _____

_____

3. **Think** about the passage. **Complete** each sentence below.

   a. A plant that does not get enough light will _____.

   b. A plant that gets just the right amount of air, light, and water will

   _____.

   c. A plant that gets too little water will _____.

Brain Builder

Imagine that you have a plant. On the back of this sheet, write a note that tells a friend how to take care of it.

Context clues, fact and opinion, main idea

What do you know about the parts of a plant?

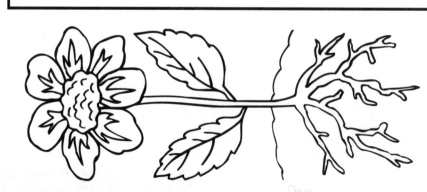

Why are roots, stems, and leaves important to plants? They each have a special purpose that helps plants <u>survive</u>.

The roots of most plants grow under the ground. They might be deep or <u>shallow</u>, but all roots help a plant in two ways. They <u>anchor</u> it in the ground. They also take in water and minerals. Some plant stems are brown and woody, and others are green and smooth. Stems carry food and minerals to different parts of a plant. The stems of most plants hold leaves. Leaves come in many different shapes and sizes. They collect light to help plants make food.

Roots, stems, and leaves are valuable to plants for <u>unique</u> reasons!

Words to Know

purpose   minerals   valuable

1. **Look** at the underlined words in the passage. **Write** each one on the line beside its meaning.

   a. special _____
   b. live _____
   c. hold _____
   d. not deep _____

2. **Write** "F" for each fact and "O" for each opinion below.

   ____ a. The stem is the most important part of a plant.
   ____ b. Roots hold a plant in the ground.
   ____ c. Leaves use light to help make food for a plant.

3. What is a good title for this passage? Why?

   _____

Brain Builder

Think about the passage. How are a plant's roots and stem alike? How are they different? Write your ideas on the back of this sheet.

PLANTS: *Functions of plant parts*

Name _____

How do seeds get scattered from place to place?

Words to Know

easily   breeze

travel

Moving On!

Do you know that seeds can travel? Seeds move about in many ways. Some seeds stick to animals' fur. They "ride" on the animals to different places. Some seeds are moved when animals eat fruit and drop its seeds.

Wind and water also move seeds. The wind can move maple tree seeds easily because they are shaped like wings. The seeds of dandelions are so <u>light</u>, they blow away in a breeze. Other seeds float on water to new places.

It is important for seeds to scatter. If all the seeds stayed in one place, they would not have enough of the things they need to grow. Be on the lookout, and you might see seeds on the move!

1. **Look** back in the passage. **Circle** the name for the flowers with seeds that the wind can move easily.

2. **Look** at the underlined word in the passage. **Circle** the letter beside its meaning below.

    a. bright   b. not heavy for its size   c. moving quickly

3. **Think** about the passage. **List** three ways that seeds are scattered.

_____

_____

Brain Builder

What do you think might happen if seeds were not scattered? Write your ideas on the back of this sheet.

What do you know about mammals' teeth?

Words to Know

prey

grind

diet

Important Tools

What important tools do all mammals have? Teeth! All mammals do not have the same kind of teeth, though. Different types of teeth help mammals eat different foods.

Wolves, tigers, and bobcats are meat eaters. A meat eater has large, pointed teeth that help it catch prey. Its front teeth cut meat from bones, and its jagged back teeth tear it. A meat eater's jaws move up and down as it chews.

Plant eaters do not chew in the same way. Giraffes, deer, cows, and other plant eaters have jaws that move from side to side and up and down. Plant eaters use their front teeth to cut plants. They grind the plants with their flat back teeth to make them easier to swallow.

A mammal's teeth tell a lot about its diet!

1. **Look** back in the passage. **Underline** the first sentence that tells why the type of teeth that a mammal has is important.

2. How many types of teeth does a meat eater have? _____

3. **Write** "P" for each plant eater and "M" for each meat eater below.

   _____ giraffe   _____ wolf   _____ bobcat

   _____ cow   _____ tiger   _____ deer

4. **Look** back at the title. Why do you think the author chose this title? _____

   _____

Some animals eat both plants and animals. What do you think their teeth look like? Why? Write your ideas on the back of this sheet.

Brain Builder

What do you know about koalas?

Words to Know

pouch

eucalyptus

grasp

Learn About Koalas!

Koalas look like bears, but they are not. They are marsupials, mammals that have pouches. After a baby koala is born, it stays in its mother's pouch until it grows more.

Koalas live in Australia where eucalyptus trees grow. The trees are their habitat. Koalas are adapted for tree life. They have good balance, so they do not usually fall from trees. Koalas are great climbers. A koala's long arms and the shape of its fingers help it grasp tree branches. Its sharp claws allow it to get a firm grip.

Eucalyptus trees are important to koalas. They eat the trees' leaves and shoots. Most koalas do not eat any other kind of food. Koalas live and play in the trees. They even sleep in them!

1. **Read** each word in the first column. **Find** its meaning in the second column. **Write** the correct letter.

   _____ marsupials
   _____ habitat
   _____ adapted
   _____ shoots

   a. place where an animal lives
   b. animals that carry their young in pouches
   c. stems or branches
   d. well fitted or suited

2. **List** two traits that help koalas live in trees. _____

   _____

3. Why are eucalyptus trees important to koalas? _____

   _____

Brain Builder

Why do you think most koalas live in Australia? Write your ideas on the back of this sheet.

Name _____

14

What traits do all mammals have?

Words to Know

echo
nocturnal
acrobat

Night Hunters

Bats look a lot like birds, but they are not. They are mammals. Like all mammals, bats are warm-blooded. This means that the air around them does not make their blood warmer or cooler. Bats and most other mammals have hair. They nurse their young. Bats are different from other mammals in one way. They are the only mammals that can fly. Bats are nocturnal. They rest during the day and come out at night.

Some bats don't see well in the dark, but they are great hunters. The bats squeak as they fly. The squeaks echo off insects and signal the bats where to fly. The bats can quickly change direction and fly toward the insects. Bats are like acrobats in the sky!

1. **Circle** each word below that tells about bats and most other mammals.

| nurse | fly | hair |
| warm-blooded | eggs | cold-blooded |

2. **Look** back in the passage. **Underline** the sentence that tells what *nocturnal* means.

3. **Read** each sentence. **Write** "T" if it is true and "F" if it is false.

a. _____ Echoes help bats find food.

b. _____ All bats see well at night.

c. _____ Bats are nocturnal birds.

d. _____ Bats make noises when they hunt.

4. Why do you think the author calls bats "acrobats in the sky"? _____

Brain Builder

How are bats like all other mammals? How are they different from some mammals? Write your answers on the back of this sheet.

Name _____

What do you know about birds?

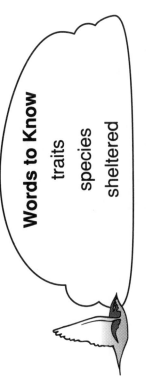

Words to Know

traits

species

sheltered

Birds, Birds, Birds!

Birds live on every continent. There are about 8,600 species of birds. Each species is different, but all birds have many of the same traits.

All birds have backbones. This means they are vertebrates. Birds are the only animals that have feathers, and some have more than 25,000 of them! All birds have beaks. Beaks help birds eat, climb, and build nests.

Birds hatch from eggs. Most eggs that are laid in nests or other sheltered places are white. Eggs that are laid in open areas are usually colored. One songbird lays a pear-shaped egg. It's a good thing, because the bird makes its nest on a mountain ledge. The egg rolls in a circle instead of falling off the ledge. Birds are amazing animals!

1. **Think** about the passage. **Write** three traits that all birds have. _____

_____

_____

2. **Look** back in the passage.

   a. **Circle** the word that means "animals with backbones."

   b. **Draw** a box around the word that means "large, main piece of earth."

3. Why do you think some bird eggs are white and some are not? _____

_____

4. **Underline** the sentence in the passage that tells the author's opinion.

Brain Builder

Do you agree with the last sentence of the passage? Why or why not? Write your answer on the back of this sheet.

How do birds use their beaks?

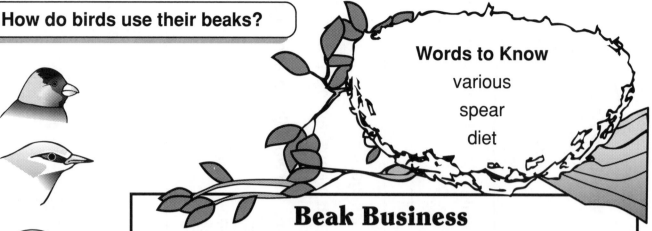

Words to Know

various

spear

diet

Beak Business

Take a close look at various birds and you'll see different beaks. A bird's beak gives a hint about the food it eats.

A finch has a beak that is shaped like a cone. It can crack food open to get to the seeds it eats. A warbler has a short, thin beak that can pick insects from plants. Another bird that has a short beak is a woodpecker. A woodpecker's beak is sharp. It uses the beak to chip wood from trees so that it can reach the insects inside. A stork has a long, sharp beak that it uses to spear fish. A vulture uses its hooked beak to tear meat.

A bird's beak is a window to its diet!

1. **Think** about the passage. **Complete** the chart.

Bird	Diet	Beak
	fish	
vulture		
		shaped like a cone
warbler		

2. Why do you think the author calls a bird's beak a "window to its diet"?

_____

_____

On the back of this sheet, draw a picture of a bird that eats seeds and animals. Explain why you drew the beak the way you did.

Brain Builder

Name _____

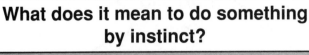

What does it mean to do something by instinct?

Words to Know
environment
saucer
resourceful

Birds do not need to be taught how to build their homes. They have an instinct for building nests. Each bird builds a nest that is right for its environment and for raising its young.

Some seabirds build nests with seaweed. An eagle uses sticks and branches to build a nest and then adds to it each year. The nest might weigh a ton. Robins use twigs and grass to make nests in the shape of a cup. A swallow uses mud to make a nest shaped like a saucer. It carries the mud in its mouth. One nest might need more than 1,000 mouthfuls of mud! When it comes to building nests, birds are very resourceful. Some storks have even used old clothes to make their nests!

1. **Think** about the passage. **Circle** the letter for the answer below that tells what *instinct* means.

   a. instant   b. natural skill   c. smell

2. **Look** back in the passage. **Underline** the sentence that tells why birds build different kinds of nests.

3. What is a good title for the passage? Why? _____

   _____

4. Why do you think the author calls birds resourceful? _____

   _____

Brain Builder

On the back of this sheet, write a "for rent" ad for a bird nest. Be sure to include what the nest is made of, where it is, and why a bird might want to live in it. Illustrate your work.

Name _____

What do you know about fish?

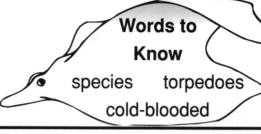

Words to Know

species   torpedoes

cold-blooded

So Many Fish!

Do you know there are more than 20,000 kinds of fish? They come in many colors. Some colors camouflage fish, or help them hide. Some colors protect fish because they warn enemies about their poison.

Fish also come in different shapes and sizes. Rays and flounder are flat. Tuna look like torpedoes. Fish can be less than an inch or more than 40 feet long!

Some species of fish have special traits. Puffers can blow up their bodies like balloons. Electric eels can make electricity.

Even though fish are different in many ways, they have a lot in common. All fish have backbones and breathe mainly with gills. Most have fins. Most are cold-blooded. All fish live mainly in the water.

Complete the outline below with information from the passage.

Fish

I. **How fish are different**

   A. Colors

      1. camouflage

      2. _____

   B. Shapes

      1. _____

      2. _____

   C. _____

      1. less than an inch long

      2. _____

   D. Traits

      1. _____

      2. _____

II. **How fish are alike**

   A. _____

   B. _____

   C. _____

   D. _____

   E. _____

How are fish like people? How are they different? Write your ideas on the back of this sheet.

Brain Builder

Name _____

Why are fish important to people?

Words to Know

food chain   balance   pollution

A Fishy Chain

What animals live in the water and help people and animals everywhere? Fish! Fish are part of many food chains. This means that a lot of people and animals depend on them. Fish are a big source of food.

Fish are important in other ways, too. They eat clams, worms, and other fish. Some fish eat plants. Fish help keep the number of plants and animals in balance. In this way they help the earth stay healthy.

Fish help scientists learn about the earth. Water pollution hurts fish. Scientists can study fish to find out whether the water is healthy. Most of the earth is water, so the health of the water tells a lot about the health of the earth.

1. **Look** back in the passage. **Underline** the sentence that tells how some fish help keep the number of plants in balance.

2. **Write** one reason from the passage that fish are important to people. _____

3. How do fish keep the earth healthy? _____

4. **Explain** how fish can tell scientists that the earth is healthy. _____

Brain Builder

How do you think the earth would be different if there were no fish? Write your thoughts on the back of this sheet.

©2001 The Education Center, Inc. • Comprehension Connections • TEC4111 • Key p. 62

19

FISH: *Importance*

Name _____

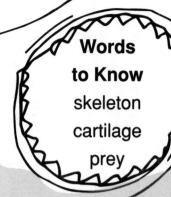

What makes sharks unique?

Words to Know
skeleton
cartilage
prey

"Sense-ational" Sharks

Sharks are not like most fish. A fish has a bony skeleton, but a shark's skeleton is made from cartilage. A fish does not sink in water even if it stays still. A shark needs to swim all the time or it will sink. Sharks are the biggest fish in the world.

One of the most special things about a shark is its senses. A shark has two tiny holes on top of its head. They help the shark hear sounds several miles away. A shark's sense of sight is strong, too. <u>It can easily spot prey in dim light.</u> A shark's sense of smell is so good that some people call sharks "swimming noses." Sharp senses make sharks great hunters!

1. What are three senses that help sharks hunt? _____

    _____

2. **Look** at the underlined sentence in the passage. What does *spot* mean?

    _____

3. Why do you think the author chose the title " 'Sense-ational' Sharks"?

    _____

    _____

4. **Circle** the words below that tell about sharks. *(Hint: There are three of them.)*

    fish   hunters   still   bony   tiny   unique

How might it be helpful for a person to have senses as sharp as a shark's? Write your ideas on the back of this sheet.

Brain Builder

What are some things that can change the earth?

Words to Know

grinds

valley

ridge

River of Ice

Picture a mountain where it is so cold, the snow never melts. Year after year, the snow piles up and gets packed into ice. The ice might become thousands of feet thick! When the ice gets very heavy, it slowly starts to move down the mountain. It becomes a glacier.

A glacier might move only 12 inches a day, but it can change the earth in big ways. A glacier cuts through a mountain and makes a valley. It picks up rocks and soil. It grinds them into small pieces as it moves. When the glacier gets to warmer ground, it melts into rivers or lakes. It leaves the rocks and soil behind in hills and ridges.

1. **Look** back in the passage. **Underline** the words that tell how fast a glacier might move.

2. **Complete** each sentence with a word below. *(Hint: You will not use one of the words.)*

ridges	grind	valley	melt	weight

a. Glaciers _____ rocks when they move down mountains.

b. The _____ of the ice and snow pulls them down the mountain.

c. Some rivers and lakes are made when glaciers _____.

d. Glaciers might leave _____ of broken rocks.

3. **Think** about the passage. What is one way that a glacier might change the earth? _____

_____

Brain Builder

How is a glacier like a river? How is it different? Write your ideas on the back of this sheet.

Context clues, main idea, sequencing

What causes an earthquake?

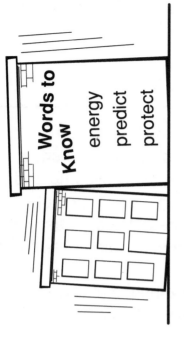

Earthquake!

Do you know that part of the earth is made of plates? They are not the kind of plates that people use for food, of course. They are large pieces of rock. The plates push against each other. Sometimes the plates get stuck, then snap. The energy from when they snap makes the ground shake. This is called an earthquake.

Many earthquakes are so small that no one feels them. Other earthquakes are much stronger and cause damage.

A lot can be done to help people stay safe during earthquakes. Scientists study earthquakes to learn more about predicting them. People can learn earthquake safety tips to protect themselves. Buildings can even be made so that they do not break during an earthquake!

Words to Know

energy

predict

protect

1. **Think** about the passage. **Number** the sentences below.

____ The plates snap and cause an earthquake.
____ The earth's plates push against each other.
____ The plates get stuck.

2. **Read** the words below. For each one, **write** the letter for its meaning.

____ protect   a. break suddenly
____ damage   b. to harm
____ energy   c. to keep from harm
____ snap   d. force

3. How can scientists who study earthquakes help people stay safe? _____

Brain Builder

Think about the passage. On the back of this sheet, write a letter that tells a friend about earthquakes.

THE CHANGING EARTH: *Earthquakes*

What do you know about volcanoes?

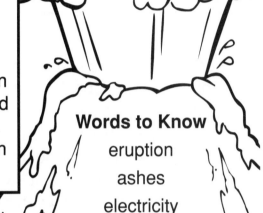

For many years, a mountain named Mount St. Helens stood quietly in the state of Washington. On May 18, 1980, it exploded like dynamite. The top of the mountain blew off! Gas and rock poured out of a vent in the mountain. Red-hot lava, or melted rock, ran down the sides. Trees were blown down and burned. Ashes fell. It was the worst volcano eruption in the United States.

Volcanoes such as Mount St. Helens are dangerous, but they can be helpful, too. They can heat water, which can be used to heat homes and make electricity. Ashes from volcanoes are good for soil, and they help plants grow. Volcanoes can also make new mountains and islands.

Words to Know

eruption

ashes

electricity

1. **Look** back in the passage. **Circle** the word that means "opening."

2. What is melted rock from a volcano called? _____

3. **Underline** the sentence in the passage that tells why a farmer might want to live near a volcano.

4. **Think** about the passage. Do you think volcanoes are more helpful or harmful? Why? _____

_____

5. What is a good title for this passage? Why? _____

_____

_____

Brain Builder

Imagine that you were a newspaper reporter on May 18, 1980. On the back of this sheet, write an article about Mount St. Helens.

Why do we need the sun?

A Special Star

Looking at stars is a fun nighttime activity. You don't need to wait until night to see one special star, though. The sun is such a bright star that you can see it during the day. Like all stars, the sun is a huge ball of burning gases. It is 93 million miles away, but it is the closest star to the earth.

The sun isn't the biggest star, but it is the most important. The sun gives people light and energy. It keeps the earth warm. It helps plants and animals grow. The sun's energy can be used to heat water and homes. All people, animals, and plants depend on the sun.

1. **Circle** the words below that tell about the sun. *(Hint: There are four of them.)*

   planet   star   hot   clouds   gas   useful

2. **Underline** the words in the passage that tell what stars are made of.

3. **Think** about the passage. Write three reasons why the sun is important.

   a. _____

   b. _____

   c. _____

4. What is another good title for the passage? Why? _____

   _____

   _____

On a separate sheet of paper, write a thank-you note to the sun for all that it does for people. Start the note "Dear Sun."

Brain Builder

What are some of Earth's characteristics?

Words to Know

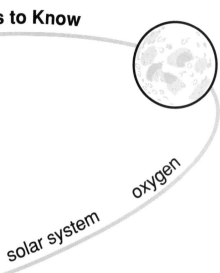

planet   solar system   oxygen

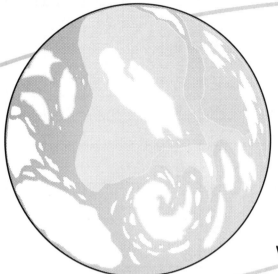

Planet Earth

What makes Earth unique? It is the only planet in the solar system that has enough oxygen for people to breathe. Earth has plenty of water, too. Water covers more than two-thirds of it.

Earth is a good distance from the sun for living things. If it were closer to the sun like Venus, it would be too hot for people, animals, or plants. If Earth were farther from the sun like Mars, it would be too cold for living things to survive. Earth is the only planet that scientists know of that has animal life.

Earth's location and its oxygen and water <u>supply</u> make it just right for plants, animals, and people!

1. **Think** about the passage. **List** three facts about Earth.

    a. _____

    _____

    b. _____

    _____

    c. _____

    _____

2. **Look** at the underlined word in the passage. **Circle** the letter for its meaning below.

    a. needs   b. distance   c. amount

3. Venus is the second planet from the sun. Mars is the fourth planet from the sun. What planet is third from the sun? _____

Brain Builder

How did you decide on your answer for number 3? Explain on the back of this sheet.

Completing a chart, details, main idea

Words to Know

poles

meteors

atmosphere

Mercury

Venus

Earth

Mars

What do you know about Mercury, Venus, and Mars?

The Earth-Like Planets

Mercury, Venus, and Mars have something in common. They are all Earth-like planets. They are small, solid, and made of rock and metal just like Earth is.

Mercury is the closest planet to the sun. It has almost no atmosphere, so it is very hot during the day and cold at night. The atmosphere is so thin that it cannot stop meteors. That is why Mercury has craters.

Venus is the second planet from the sun. It is hotter than Mercury. It has a lot of clouds. Its atmosphere is thick and poisonous.

Mars, the fourth planet, is covered with red dust. Its atmosphere is too thin for people to breathe. Mars is cold. It has frozen water at its poles like Earth does.

1. Why do you think Mercury, Venus, and Mars are called Earth-like planets?

   _____

2. **Underline** the sentence in the passage that tells how Mars and Earth are alike.

3. **Think** about the passage. **Complete** the chart.

Planet	Order From the Sun	Temperature	Atmosphere	Other Information
Earth	third	mild	people can breathe	has living things
			thin, people can't breathe	
Venus	first			

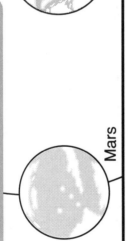

Brain Builder

Think about the passage. If you could visit one of the Earth-like planets, which one would you choose? Why? Write your answers on the back of this sheet.

SOLAR SYSTEM: *Mercury, Venus, & Mars*

Words to Know
spread   weight
represent

Soda, Anyone?

Think about a glass of soda. It takes up space and has weight. That means it is made of matter. It doesn't represent just one kind of matter, though. It represents three!

The soda is a liquid. It always takes the same amount of space, but its shape can change when it is poured into different containers. The soda bubbles are a gas. Heating or cooling a gas changes how much space it takes. Soda bubbles, air, and other gases spread to fill any space. The glass is a solid. A solid has its own shape, and it is not easy to change it.

The next time you see a glass of soda, think about the three states of matter!

1. What is the same about each of the three states of matter?

   _____

2. **Think** about the states of matter. For each group of words, **draw** a line through the word that does not belong.

box	soda bubbles	notebook	skateboard
juice	air	lemonade	ice cube
car	gravy	glue	river

3. How is a solid different from a liquid? _____

   _____

Brain Builder

Imagine that you need to teach a classmate about matter. What would you say or do? Write your thoughts on the back of this sheet.

What are some ways to define matter?

Words to Know
properties   definite
depend

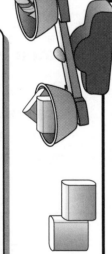

Measuring Matter

A feather, a bowl of cake batter, and the air inside a balloon are alike in one way. They are all made of matter. Each of them has properties that make it <u>unique</u>, though. Two properties of matter are mass and volume.

Mass is how much matter an object has. The weight of an object depends on how much mass it has. A balance or scale can <u>measure</u> mass. A bag of flour is sold by mass.

Volume is how much <u>space</u> an object takes. A solid and a liquid both have <u>definite</u> volumes, but a gas does not. A gallon of milk is sold by volume.

Mass and volume are two handy ways to <u>describe</u> matter!

1. **Look** at the underlined words in the passage. **Write** each one beside its meaning below.

a. tell the size or amount _____
b. exact _____
c. special _____
d. tell about _____
e. area _____

2. **Write** "T" for each true sentence and "F" for each false sentence below.

a. ____ An object that takes up a lot of space has a large volume.
b. ____ Mass and volume are kinds of measurements.
c. ____ All matter has a definite volume.

3. Which do you think has a greater mass: a feather or a bowl of cake batter? Why? _____

Brain Builder

Why do you think the author calls volume and mass handy ways to describe matter? Write your ideas on the back of this sheet.

What are some things that get hot quickly?

Words to Know
conduct

metal

plastic

Heat on the Move

Do you know that heat moves? It can even travel through solid objects! When heat moves this way, it is called conduction. Some kinds of matter conduct heat well. Other kinds do not.

A metal pan conducts heat well. Heat from a gas stove moves through it to cook the food it holds. An electric iron also conducts heat well. It can be used to press clothes. Heat from fire can move through a grill to cook meat.

Heat does not move through wood and plastic quickly. These materials do not conduct heat well, so they are good for things such as the handles for cooking pots.

There are many important uses for both good and poor heat conductors!

1. Why do you think the author chose the title "Heat on the Move"?

_____

2. Heat comes from many different places. **Write** one heat source named in the passage. _____

3. **Look** back in the passage. **Circle** the two poor heat conductors.

4. **Draw** a line from each sentence beginning to the best ending.

   a. A wooden spoon is good to use when cooking •
   b. When heat passes through something •
   c. A metal pot heats quickly •

   • it is called conduction.
   • because it is a good heat conductor.
   • because it is a poor heat conductor.

Brain Builder

On the back of this sheet, use what you learned about conduction to describe and draw two new kinds of cooking pans and utensils.

What do you know about energy?

Words to Know

form

electricity

sources

Energy Is Everywhere!

What do people use every day? Energy! People use energy at home, school, and work. They use it to turn on lights, heat homes, and make cars go. People and animals need energy to move and grow. They cannot live without it.

Energy comes in forms such as heat, light, and electricity. Energy can change forms. The electricity from lightning turns into heat and light energy. It becomes sound energy when it makes thunder.

The sun, wind, and water are energy sources. Most of Earth's energy comes from the sun. In one day, the sun can make all the energy humans need for one year! Maybe someday people will find a way to collect all of the sun's energy.

1. **List** two uses for energy from the passage. _____

_____

2. **Complete** each sentence with a word below. *(Hint: You will not use one of the words.)*

sun	energy	water	electricity	sound

a. Heat, light, _____, and electric energy come from lightning and thunder.

b. Energy comes from _____ and the sun.

c. The _____ is Earth's biggest source of energy.

d. Dogs and cats cannot live without _____.

3. Why might people want to find ways to collect and use the sun's energy?

_____

Think about the passage. How might your life be different if there were no electric energy? Write your ideas on the back of this sheet.

Brain Builder

Cause and effect, context clues, drawing conclusions

Why does a hat help keep a person warm in cold weather?

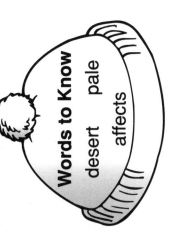

Hot and Cold

Imagine that you leave a bowl of hot soup on a table. The heat from the soup moves to the room. The soup gets cold. This change happens because heat <u>transfers</u> from warmer to cooler places.

The same thing happens when a person goes outside in cold weather. His body heat <u>escapes</u> to the cold air. If the person wears a hat, he keeps in some of the heat.

Sometimes people or animals do not want to keep heat in. They want to keep heat out. The desert fox's <u>pale</u> fur does not <u>absorb</u> much heat. It slows down the transfer of heat from the air to the fox.

Heat transfer <u>affects</u> people and animals in important ways!

Words to Know

desert   pale

affects

1. **Look** at the underlined words in the passage. **Write** each one on the line beside its meaning below.

a. goes _____

b. take in _____

c. moves from one thing to another _____

d. not dark _____

2. **Read** each pair of sentences below. For each one, **write** "C" beside the cause and "E" beside the effect.

a. ____ The desert fox stays cool during the day.
   ____ The desert fox has pale fur.

b. ____ The boy wears mittens outside.
   ____ The boy's body heat does not escape quickly.

c. ____ The cold soda is in the warm room.
   ____ The soda becomes warm.

Brain Builder

Think about the passage. If a person wants to warm up on a sunny day, should he wear light- or dark-colored clothes? Why? Write your answers on the back of this sheet.

©2001 The Education Center, Inc. • *Comprehension Connections* • TEC4111 • Key p. 63

ENERGY, LIGHT, & HEAT: *Heat transfer*

Name _____

How are shadows made?

Words to Know

block   observe   sundial

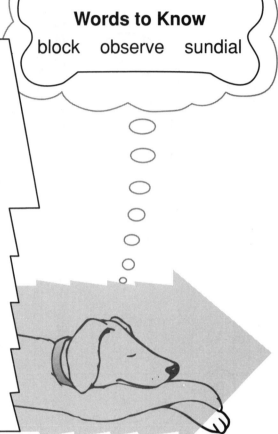

Sunny Day Wonders

On a sunny day, you can see a lot of shadows. You might even see your own! Two things are needed to make a shadow. Light is one of them. An opaque object is the other. An opaque object <u>blocks</u> light. People, animals, books, and cars are all opaque.

The shape of a shadow looks like the object that makes it, but its size can change. If an object moves away from the light, the shadow gets smaller. It shrinks because the object does not block as much light.

Shadows are not just fun to observe; they are helpful, too. They can tell people how high the sun is in the sky. The shadows on a sundial can even help people tell time!

1. **Look** at the underlined word in the passage. **Circle** the letter for its meaning below.

    a. wooden cubes   b. stops   c. shapes

2. **Write** "T" beside each true sentence and "F" beside each false sentence below.

    a. _____ Any object can make a shadow if light shines on it.
    b. _____ Rabbits, horses, and dogs are opaque.
    c. _____ The size of a shadow always stays the same.

3. What would happen to a box's shadow if the box were moved closer to the light? _____

4. **Underline** the sentence in the passage that tells the author's opinion.

If you went outside on a cloudy day, would you see shadows? Why or why not? Write your ideas on the back of this sheet.

Brain Builder

Name _____

What do you know about Native American homes from long ago?

Words to Know

depended

planks

resources

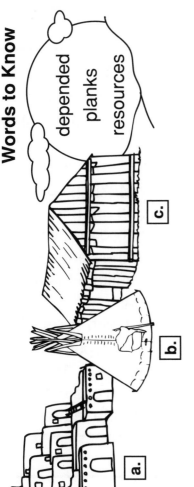

a.

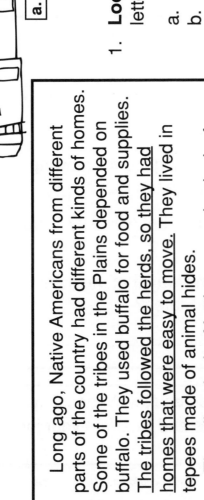

b.

c.

Long ago, Native Americans from different parts of the country had different kinds of homes. Some of the tribes in the Plains depended on buffalo. They used buffalo for food and supplies. The tribes followed the herds, so they had homes that were easy to move. They lived in tepees made of animal hides.

The tribes in the Northwest made planks from trees. They used them to make large homes. The homes were so big, 50 people could live in one of them!

In the Southwest, tribes made homes from clay bricks called adobe. The homes were many stories high.

Each region's resources made a big difference in the lives of Native Americans!

1. **Look** at the underlined sentence in the passage. **Circle** the letter for the answer below that tells what *herds* means.

    a. listened
    b. brings together
    c. groups of animals

2. **Think** about the passage. **Look** at the pictures. **Write** each letter on the correct line below.

    _____ Northwest   _____ Plains   _____ Southwest

3. Why do you think the author says that each region's resources made a big difference to Native Americans?

    _____

Brain Builder

What is a good title for the passage? Why? Write your thoughts on the back of this sheet.

What are customs?

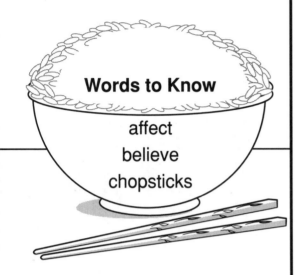

Words to Know

affect

believe

chopsticks

Dinnertime!

All around the world, people gather to eat. Regions and customs affect what people eat and how their food is served.

The land in <u>China</u> is good for growing rice. Rice is part of many meals. In <u>Mexico</u>, corn is a main crop. A lot of Mexican foods are made with it.

People in <u>Japan</u> believe that red and white bring luck. On New Year's Day they eat red and white foods. In <u>Russia</u> people believe that honey cake will bring a sweet new year.

People in many countries eat with forks. The people in China and Japan use chopsticks instead. Plates and bowls are used in the United States. In some parts of India, the custom is different. Food is served on banana leaves!

1. **Look** at the underlined words in the passage. **Use** each one to complete a sentence below. *(Hint: Use each word only once.)*

    a. People in _____ believe that eating red and white foods will bring luck in the new year.
    b. Rice is often served in _____.
    c. The land in _____ is good for growing corn.
    d. A sweet dessert is served on New Year's Day in _____.

2. **Underline** the sentence in the passage that tells why people might eat different things in different countries.

3. **Think** about the passage. What is one way that mealtime in China is different from mealtime in the United States? _____

    _____

Imagine that a friend from Japan visits you on New Year's Day. What foods would you serve? Why? Write and illustrate your ideas on the back of this sheet.

Brain Builder

What do you think games are like in other countries?

Words to Know
popular   object
piñata

Let's Play!

People everywhere love to play games! In the United States, many people enjoy field hockey. A similar game in Ireland is called hurling. The players use a leather ball and sticks that are more curved than hockey sticks.

Some games have different names in different countries. Blind Man's Bluff is one of them. In Greece and Spain it is called Blind Cat. In Austria it is called Blind Cow.

Some games start in one country, then spread to other parts of the world. The game of piñata is from Mexico. Now it is popular in many countries. A piñata is a container filled with treats. The object of the game is to break it and get the treats inside.

Games are fun all over the world!

1. **Read** each word in the first column below. **Write** the correct letter in the blank beside it to show its meaning in the passage.

   _____ curved   a. goal
   _____ similar   b. rounded
   _____ object   c. material made from animal skin
   _____ leather   d. almost the same
   _____ spread   e. become known

2. **Look** back in the passage. **Underline** the word for the game that is almost like field hockey.

3. What do piñata players try to do? _____

_____

Brain Builder

How do you think games like piñata spread to other parts of the world? Write your ideas on the back of this sheet.

What do you know about colonial times?

What jobs did people have during colonial times? Some people were farmers. A colonial farmer planted and harvested crops by hand. Some people were blacksmiths. They made pots, nails, tools, and horseshoes. There were no dentists, so blacksmiths also pulled teeth!

A cooper was another important colonial worker. He made barrels to hold food and water. Cobblers, or shoemakers, made, mended, and sold shoes. To make their jobs easier, cobblers made left and right shoes the same.

Today some people have jobs that are like jobs from long ago. Machines make their work faster, though. Machines can help plant seeds, harvest crops, and sew clothes. They can even help make left and right shoes!

Words to Know

harvest

barrel

mend

1. What is a good title for the passage?
   Circle the letter for the best answer below.

   a. Farming Long Ago   c. Jobs Long Ago and Today
   b. Left or Right?   d. Machines Are Great!

2. **Write** the letters to match the jobs and items. **Use** each letter only once.

   _____ cobbler   a. crops
   _____ farmer   b. nails
   _____ cooper   c. barrels
   _____ blacksmith   d. shoes

3. What is one way that colonial jobs are different from today's jobs?

   _____

Look back at your answer for number 1. On the back of this sheet, explain how you decided on your answer.

Brain Builder

What are some tools for telling time?

Words to Know

hourglass

shadow

electric

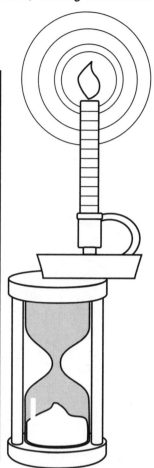

Right on Time!

Candles, sand, and the sun were used to tell time long ago. Some people made marks along candles to show the hours. To tell the time, they checked to see how far down a candle had burned.

An hourglass was another tool for measuring time. An hourglass holds sand. It takes a certain amount of time for the sand to pass from one part of the hourglass to the other.

A sundial is a disk marked in hours almost like a clock face is. When the sun shines on it, a shadow points to the hour.

Now people use watches, electric clocks, and many other kinds of clocks. They are much more exact than the clocks from the past!

1. **Look** back in the passage. **Circle** the word that means "round, flat object."

2. **Complete** each sentence with a word below. *(Hint: You will not use two of the words.)*

sand	shadow	exact	burning	watches	hourglass

   a. An _____ holds sand.
   b. Some people told time by _____ a marked candle.
   c. A candle clock is not as _____ as an electric clock.
   d. To read a sundial, you must look at the _____ on it.

3. What might be a problem with using a sundial to tell time? **Explain.**

   _____

   _____

Brain Builder

Do you think an hourglass or a sundial is a better tool for measuring time? Why? Write your answers on the back of this sheet.

Context clues, drawing conclusions, sequencing

How did people communicate many years ago?

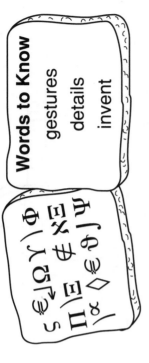

Words to Know

gestures

details

invent

The Story of Writing

Thousands of years ago, people did not have a way to write. They talked or made gestures instead. People often forgot details. They needed a better way to share their thoughts.

People began to draw pictures to communicate. They drew pictures on clay, leaves, and wood before paper was invented. Later people started to use symbols. Symbols are signs that stand for other things. After a while, alphabets were invented. People used the letters for sounds or parts of words. They put the letters together to make words.

Now there are alphabets all over the world. The longest one has 74 letters. The shortest one has just 11 letters!

1. **Look** at the underlined sentence in the passage. What does *signs* mean? **Circle** the letter below to show your answer.

   a. writes your name

   b. marks used in place of words

   c. posters with writing

2. **Number** the words below to show how the way that people communicate has changed over time.

   ____ a. pictures

   ____ b. alphabet

   ____ c. symbols

3. Do you think alphabets or pictures are a better way to write? Why? _____

Brain Builder

Think about the passage. Why do you think there is more than one alphabet? Write your ideas on the back of this sheet.

THEN & NOW: *Writing*

Name _____

What do you know about geography?

A Look at Land

What is the land like where you live? The answer is part of geography! Geography is the study of the earth's surface, its climate, and its resources. Most of the earth's surface is covered with water. The rest has many different landforms.

The biggest pieces of land on the earth are called continents. There are seven of them. The earth also has smaller pieces of land that are surrounded by water. They are called islands. A peninsula looks almost like an island. It is a landform that has water on nearly all sides.

Mountains and valleys are two other kinds of landforms. Mountains are large hills. Valleys are the low spots between them.

Look around your region. You might see these and other landforms!

1. **Read** each word in the first column. **Write** the correct letter to show its meaning.

   _____ peninsula   a. land with water all around it
   _____ continent   b. low land between mountains
   _____ mountain   c. land with water on almost all sides
   _____ valley   d. one of the seven largest pieces of land on earth
   _____ island   e. big hill

2. How much of the earth is covered by water? **Circle** the best answer below.

   less than half   half   more than half

3. **Think** about the passage. What do you think *landform* means?

   _____

   _____

Brain Builder

Draw and label a picture of an island and a picture of a peninsula on the back of this sheet. Then write how an island and a peninsula are alike.

What are natural resources?

Words to Know

treasure
oxygen
community

Treasures From the Land

Earth is filled with treasures! They are not the kind of treasures that are hidden in chests. They are natural resources. Air, water, and land are natural resources. Plants and animals are, too.

The natural resources are different from place to place. Some regions have a lot of trees. Trees give people oxygen and shade. They can also be used to make lumber and paper. Some towns have lakes. The lakes might give people water to drink or fish to catch. Other places might have soil that is good for growing crops. Farmers can grow and sell the crops to people who live where the soil is not as good.

Natural resources help make every community special!

1. **Read** each list of words below. **Draw** a line through the word in each list that is not a natural resource.

air	blanket	sunlight	forests	stove
candle	pond	soil	books	carrots
cow	mountain	bike	fish	river

2. Why are trees an important natural resource? _____

_____

3. **Look** back at the title. Why do you think the author chose this title? _____

_____

On the back of this sheet, draw and label three natural resources from the region where you live. Explain how they are important to people.

Brain
Builder

Context clues, details, main idea

Words to Know

tool

distance

landforms

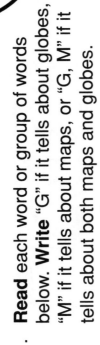

How are maps and globes used?

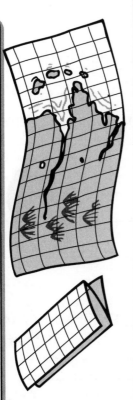

What are two great tools for planning trips? Maps and globes! They both show places and the distance between them. Sometimes it is better to use a map, and other times a globe is more helpful.

A globe is a model of the earth that shows its true shape. It is good to use when you want to see the whole earth at once. A map is a drawing on a flat surface. It might show the entire earth or only part of it. Many maps can be folded and are easy to carry.

Maps can be drawn to show many things. They might show landforms or weather in different regions. You could even draw a map to show where things are on your desktop!

1. **Read** each word or group of words below. **Write** "G" if it tells about globes, "M" if it tells about maps, or "G, M" if it tells about both maps and globes.

   a. _____ flat

   b. _____ shows the whole earth

   c. _____ helpful

   d. _____ round

   e. _____ might show only part of the earth

2. **Look** back in the passage.

   a. **Circle** the word that means "a copy of something larger."

   b. **Underline** the word that means "whole."

3. What is a good title for the passage? Why?

   _____

Brain Builder

On the back of this sheet, write about a time that would be good to use a map. Then write about a time that a globe would be more useful.

©2001 The Education Center, Inc. • *Comprehension Connections* • TEC4111 • Key p. 63

GEOGRAPHY: *Maps & globes*

What are some jobs that are important to communities?

Words to Know
skills   trained
depend

Jobs to Count On!

Imagine that you have to make your clothes, fill the cavities in your teeth, and take care of anything else you need all by yourself. It would be impossible to learn how to do so many things!

Luckily, many people learn special skills. Other people can depend on them to do certain jobs. Think about a postal worker. His mail truck is made by people who work in factories. Road crews keep the streets he drives on in good shape. Police officers are trained to make sure that the roads stay safe. The postal worker depends on these people so that he can do his job. People depend on him to deliver their mail.

Every job helps people get the things they need and want!

1. **Look** back in the passage. **Circle** the word that means "groups of people working together."

2. **List** three jobs from the passage that people might be trained to do.

   _____

3. **Think** about the passage. **Write** how things might be for postal workers and other people if each sentence below were true.

   a. There are very few road crews. _____

   _____

   b. No one is trained to work in truck factories. _____

   _____

On the back of this sheet, list three jobs in your community. Explain how people depend on someone to do each job.

Brain Builder

What does it mean to trade something?

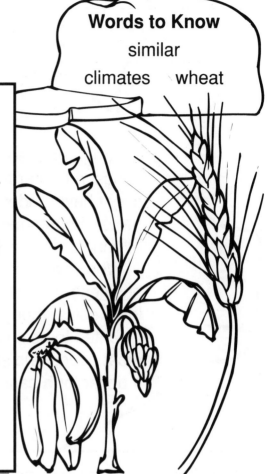

Let's Trade!

What would you do if you had two of the same baseball card? You might give one to a friend and ask the friend for a card that you do not have. That would be a trade. Many countries make trades in a similar way. One country gives something to another country and gets something it wants in return.

One food that the United States trades for is bananas. Bananas do not grow in the United States. They grow only in warmer climates.

Wheat and many other foods grow well in parts of the United States. Other countries that cannot grow enough wheat trade with the United States for it.

Trade helps people all over the world!

1. **Explain** in your own words what *trade* means. _____

   _____

2. Why does the United States trade for bananas? _____

   _____

3. **Circle** the letter for the words below that best complete this sentence: The author wrote this passage to

   a. ask for new baseball cards.
   b. tell what kind of climate bananas need.
   c. explain what trade is and why it is important.
   d. get people to trade with their friends.

Brain Builder

On the back of this sheet, explain why it is important for countries to make trades.

How can a person tell the value of something?

Words to Know

barter   weaver

services

Money Matters

Long ago, people did not have money. People bartered for things. A farmer might have traded corn for cloth. A <u>weaver</u> might have traded cloth for food. It was not always easy to barter. Sometimes people could not agree about the <u>value</u> of things.

When coins were invented, it became easier for people to do <u>business</u>. The value of one coin was clear. It is hard to carry a lot of coins, though, because they are heavy. Dollar bills were invented to help with this problem. They are much lighter. Now most <u>goods</u> and <u>services</u> have prices. It is a lot easier to pay a dollar for a candy bar than to barter a sheep for it!

1. **Look** back in the passage. **Underline** the first sentence that tells how people used to get the things they needed.

2. **Look** at the underlined words in the passage. **Write** each one on the correct line below.

    a. buying and selling   _____

    b. worth   _____

    c. things that are sold   _____

    d. person who makes cloth   _____

    e. work done for other people   _____

3. Why might a farmer have used corn to make trades instead of wood or tools?

    _____

Look at the last sentence in the passage. Do you agree with the author? Why or why not? Write your thoughts on the back of this sheet.

Brain Builder

Name _____

What do you know about elections?

Words to Know

citizen

leader

political

Vote!

United States citizens help decide who will lead the government. They choose the leaders through elections. The biggest election is for the president.

An election for president is held every four years. A lot of work is done before Election Day. <u>Each political party chooses a candidate.</u> The candidates campaign. Each candidate tells the voters why he or she would be a good president.

On the Tuesday after the first Monday in November, each voter casts a ballot for his favorite candidate. Then, through a special system, the states cast votes. The candidate who gets the most state votes is named the president of the United States!

1. **Look** back at the underlined sentence in the passage.
   Circle the letter for the answer below that tells what *party* means.

   a. special time to have fun
   b. celebrate with friends
   c. group of people who share political ideas

2. **Use** the words below to complete the sentences. *(Hint: You will not use one of the words.)*

election	president	candidate	citizens	casts

   a. When a person votes, he _____ a ballot.
   b. A person who tries to win an _____ is a candidate.
   c. The _____ vote for a president every four years.
   d. A campaign is a time for people to decide which _____ they like.

3. What is an election? _____

Brain Builder

Do you think campaigns are important to elections? Why or why not? Write your ideas on the back of this sheet.

Name _____ *Comparison and contrast, details, drawing conclusions*

Who are the leaders of the United States government?

Government Leaders

Running the United States government is a huge job! It is so big that it is shared by three levels: local, state, and national. Each level has its own leader. The leader works to meet the needs and wants of the citizens.

The leader at the local level is the mayor. The mayor works in city hall. One of the mayor's jobs is to manage the police and fire departments. The governor is the leader at the state level. The governor works in the state capitol. He helps decide things such as how much state money to spend on schools. The national leader, the president, works in Washington, DC. He is the leader of the entire country.

Words to Know
level
manage
departments

Ms. Ima Mayor

1. **Draw** a line from each leader in the left column to the matching word in the right column.

    a. mayor •   • state
    b. governor •   • national
    c. president •   • local

2. **Look** back in the passage. **Follow** the directions below.

    a. **Circle** the words that tell where the governor works.
    b. **Draw** a box around the words that tell where the mayor works.

3. **Imagine** that you have an idea for a new state song. Who would be the best leader to tell about it: the mayor, governor, or president? Why? _____

    _____

Think about the passage. How are a governor and a president alike? Different? Write your ideas on the back of this sheet.

Brain Builder

Name _____

What are some of the president's duties?

Words to Know

powerful   ceremonies

armed forces

1. **Read** the words in the first column. For each one, **write** the letter for its meaning.

_____ often   a. follow
_____ duties   b. passed
_____ obey   c. many times
_____ approved   d. jobs

2. **List** two of the president's duties from the passage.

_____

_____

3. **Write** "F" for each fact and "O" for each opinion below.

a. _____ The most important part of the president's job is to help make laws.

b. _____ Many people invite the president to celebrations.

c. _____ The president should throw the first ball of the baseball season.

A Powerful Person

What is it like to be one of the most powerful people in the world? The president of the United States knows. He is the leader of the country. The president lives and works in the White House. He often works in a room called the Oval Office.

The president has many important duties. One of his duties is to work with the leaders of other countries. He is also the commander in chief. This means he is in charge of the armed forces. The president helps make sure that people obey the national laws, and he works with people to get new laws approved. The president goes to many ceremonies and celebrations. Sometimes he even throws the first ball of the baseball season!

Brain Builder

Think about the passage. Would you like to have the president's job? Why or why not? Write your ideas on the back of this sheet.

©2001 The Education Center, Inc. • *Comprehension Connections* • TEC4111 • Key p. 64

CIVICS & GOVERNMENT: *Presidential responsibilities*

47

Name _____

48

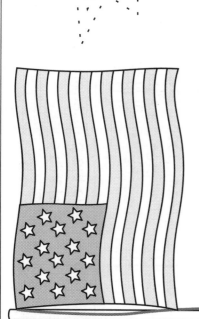

What does it mean to be proud?

Words to Know
anthem Great Britain
bombard

America's Song

In 1814 America was at war with Great Britain. The countries had been fighting for more than two years. In one battle the British bombarded an American fort. The attack lasted all day and most of the night.

An American lawyer named Francis Scott Key was there. He watched the battle from a ship. In the morning, he saw the American flag still flying over the fort. Great Britain had lost the battle! Key was proud of his country. He wrote a song to celebrate the win. The song is called "The Star-Spangled Banner." Today it is America's national anthem. Americans sing it to show pride for their country.

1. **Number** the sentences below in the correct order.

___ "The Star-Spangled Banner" becomes a national anthem.

___ Great Britain attacks an American fort.

___ America wins a battle against Great Britain.

___ Francis Scott Key writes "The Star-Spangled Banner."

2. How did Francis Scott Key know that America had won the battle? _____

3. Why did Francis Scott Key write "The Star-Spangled Banner"? _____

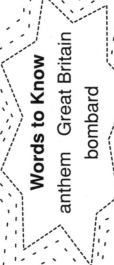

Brain Builder

Think about a time that you felt proud. Write about it on the back of this sheet.

©2001 The Education Center, Inc. • *Comprehension Connections* • TEC4111 • Key p. 64

THE UNITED STATES: *"The Star-Spangled Banner"*

Name _____

Words to Know

soldier   memorial   observe

What makes a person a hero?

Honoring America's Soldiers

America's soldiers have an important and dangerous job. They <u>protect</u> the United States. Sometimes they need to fight for the country's freedom. Some soldiers die in wars. Memorial Day <u>honors</u> all American soldiers who die in <u>battle</u>. This holiday is also called Poppy Day.

People in a lot of states observe Memorial Day on the last Monday in May. It is a special day. Schools close. Parades are held. People put flags and flowers on soldiers' graves. Many of them use red flowers called poppies to decorate the graves. Some <u>ports</u> honor the soldiers who died at sea. They float small ships filled with flowers. People will not forget the heroes who give their lives for America!

1. **Look** at the underlined words in the passage. On each line below, **write** the letter of the answer that has the same meaning.

   ____ ports   a. guard
   ____ honors   b. fight
   ____ protect   c. respects
   ____ battle   d. harbor towns

2. **Think** about the passage. **Write** one way that people observe Memorial Day. _____

3. **Write** "F" for each fact and "O" for each opinion below.

   a. ____ Memorial Day is observed in the spring.
   b. ____ Soldiers protect the United States.
   c. ____ Memorial Day parades are fun to watch.
   d. ____ Memorial Day is the most important holiday.

Brain Builder

How is Memorial Day like the Fourth of July? How is it different? Write your ideas on the back of this sheet.

©2001 The Education Center, Inc. • *Comprehension Connections* • TEC4111 • Key p. 64

THE UNITED STATES: *Memorial Day*

49

Context clues, details, main idea

What is freedom?

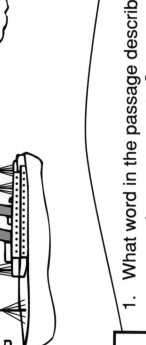

Words to Know

immigrant   official

citizen

Gateway to Freedom

In New York Harbor, close to the Statue of Liberty, is an island named Ellis Island. It used to be a very busy place. Ellis Island was the first stop for many people who moved to America. Many of the immigrants were poor. Many of them were unhappy. They wanted to be free. They wanted to be American citizens.

Thousands of people came to the island on some days! After they arrived, they saw doctors and officials. The doctors made sure the people were healthy. The officials made sure they were safe.

Now there is a museum on Ellis Island. It honors all the people who came to America to start new lives.

1. What word in the passage describes a person who comes to a new country? _____

2. **Complete** the sentences below with words from the passage.

    a. Ellis Island is in _____.
    b. The immigrants lined up to see _____ and officials.

3. Why did many people choose to come to America? _____

4. **Look** back in the passage. **Underline** the sentence that tells what you would see if you visited Ellis Island today.

Brain Builder

Why do you think the author chose the title "Gateway to Freedom"? Write your thoughts on the back of this sheet.

THE UNITED STATES: *Ellis Island*

Name _____

What does it mean to be gifted?

Words to Know

genius   symphony

opera

A Musical Gift

About 200 years ago, there lived a child named Wolfgang Amadeus Mozart. He had a special <u>gift</u> for music. He was a musical genius.

When Mozart was four years old, he learned to play a keyboard instrument called a harpsichord. Mozart could write, or compose, music at age five. When he was six years old, Mozart performed for the royal family. Later, he went on concert tours. He performed for a lot of people.

Mozart wrote and played music all his life. He wrote operas, symphonies, and church music. He wrote more than 600 pieces of music before he died at age 35. People everywhere remember Mozart as one of the best composers of all time.

1. Why was Mozart called a musical genius? _____

    _____

    _____

2. **Look** back in the passage. **Circle** the name of the instrument that Mozart played when he was a child.

3. **Look** at the underlined word in the passage. **Circle** the letter for its meaning below.

    a. present   c. give
    b. talent   d. surprise

4. **Think** about the passage. **Circle** the words below that tell about Mozart. *(Hint: There are three of them.)*

    musical   captain   composer   gifted   singer   mayor

Brain Builder

On the back of this sheet, make an ad for one of Mozart's concerts. Be sure to write who he is and the kind of music he will play.

Name _____

52

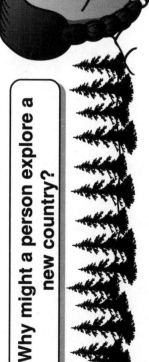

Why might a person explore a new country?

Words to Know

communicate

Sacagawea *(sah kah guh WEE uh)*

Native American

A Native American Leader

About 200 years ago, people did not know much about the United States. In 1804 a group of men set out to explore part of it. They were led by two men named Lewis and Clark.

It was not easy for Lewis and Clark to communicate with the Native Americans they met along the way. A Native American woman named Sacagawea traveled with them and helped.

Sacagawea gathered food for the men during the long, hard journey. When the explorers met a band of Shoshone people, Sacagawea talked to the tribe. She helped the tribe understand that the explorers were friendly. Sacagawea got horses from the Shoshone people for the explorers. Sacagawea helped make the trip a success.

1. **Think** about the passage. **Write** one way that Sacagawea helped the explorers. _____

2. What does *band* mean in the underlined sentence? **Circle** the letter for the correct answer.

   a. a strip of cloth   b. a group   c. a circle

3. **Circle** the word in the passage that means "trip."

4. **Write** "F" for each fact and "O" for each opinion below.

   a. _____ Sacagawea knew how to speak the Shoshone language.

   b. _____ The Shoshone tribe gave the explorers horses.

   c. _____ The explorers traveled through pretty mountain trails.

   d. _____ Native American languages are hard to understand.

Brain Builder

Imagine that Sacagawea had not gone with Lewis and Clark. How might their trip have been different? Write your ideas on the back of this sheet.

©2001 The Education Center, Inc. • *Comprehension Connections* • TEC4111 • Key p. 64

HISTORICAL FIGURES: *Sacagawea*

Name _____

What do you know about slavery?

Words to Know
forced
freedom
escape

A Fight for Freedom

Harriet Tubman was born a slave in the early 1800s. She was forced to work long hours in Maryland fields. She was not treated well. Harriet wanted a better life for herself. She wanted to be free.

In 1849 Harriet escaped from slavery by the Underground Railroad. The Railroad was a system of hiding places called stations. People called conductors helped slaves escape.

After she was free, Harriet became a conductor to help other slaves. It was dangerous for Harriet. A lot of people wanted to capture her. People who helped slaves escape were punished. That did not stop Harriet. She returned to Maryland many times and helped free about 300 slaves. Harriet Tubman was a brave leader in the fight against slavery!

1. **Number** the sentences below in the correct order.

   _____ Harriet decided to help other slaves escape.
   _____ About 300 slaves became free because of Harriet's help.
   _____ Harriet escaped from slavery.
   _____ Harriet worked in fields as a slave.

2. **Read** each sentence below. **Write** "T" for each true sentence and "F" for each false sentence.

   a. _____ The Underground Railroad hid trains.
   b. _____ Harriet showed many slaves the way to freedom.
   c. _____ The slave owners treated Harriet kindly.

3. Why do you think the author calls Harriet Tubman brave? _____

_____

Brain Builder

What is another good title for this passage? Write and explain your ideas on the back of this sheet.

What do you know about plows?

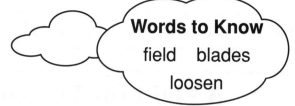

Words to Know

field   blades

loosen

Imagine digging up a huge field to get it ready for planting. It would be hard work! Luckily, most farmers do not need to dig fields by hand. They can use plows instead. Plows loosen soil, which makes it easier to plant seeds. Plants grow faster in plowed soil because the soil has more air.

Thousands of years ago, branches shaped like forks were used as plows. Farmers used the branches to break up soil. Later wooden, iron, and steel plows were invented. These plows are pulled by horses, mules, or oxen. Some have blades that cut and lift the soil. Today many farmers use tractors to pull plows. Tractor plows are handy for getting the ground ready for planting!

1. In your own words, **write** how a plow is used in planting. _____

_____

2. **Underline** the sentence in the passage that tells why plants grow well in plowed soil.

3. **Read** the sentences below. **Write** "F" for each fact and "O" for each opinion.

    a. _____   It is easier to plant seeds in soil that has been plowed than in soil that has not.

    b. _____   Tractor plows are better than plows that are pulled by horses.

    c. _____   Some of the first plows were made from trees.

4. What is a good title for this passage? Why? _____

_____

On the back of this sheet, make an ad for a plow. Be sure to write two reasons why the plow would be helpful to a farmer.

Brain Builder

Words to Know

reasons

equipment

health

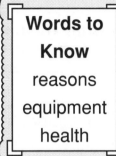

Why might people want to take photos?

Smile for the Camera!

"Say *cheese!*" When you hear this, you know that someone is using a camera! People use cameras to take photos for a lot of different reasons. Some people take photos of friends and families. The photos help them recall events and people. Some cameras can take photos of the ocean bottom or of places beyond the moon. Scientists study the photos to learn about these places. Some cameras can take photos inside people's bodies. The photos help doctors learn about the people's health.

Long ago cameras cost a lot and it took a lot of equipment and skill to use them. Now many people can afford cameras. Cameras are easier and faster to use. Some cameras can even make photos in just 15 seconds!

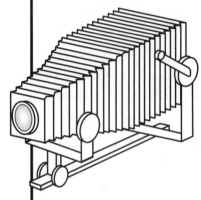

1. **Match** each word from the passage with its definition.

   _____ beyond   a. talent or training
   _____ events   b. past
   _____ skill   c. have enough money for
   _____ recall   d. remember
   _____ afford   e. things that happen

2. **Think** about the passage. **List** two ways that people might learn from photos.

   _____

   _____

3. How are cameras today different from cameras long ago? _____

   _____

Brain Builder

How do you think your life would be different if cameras had never been invented? Write your ideas on the back of this sheet.

Name _____

In what ways do people use computers?

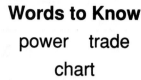

Words to Know

power   trade

chart

Computer Age

Computers have come a long way! About 40 years ago, computers were as big as a room. Today some computers can fit on desktops or on laps. Some can even fit in people's hands! Even though today's computers are smaller, they have more power.

People use computers for work and play. They can also use them to <u>communicate with</u> people all over the world. A class in the United States can use a computer to trade pictures and letters with a class in Japan. A student in Alaska can use a computer to chart the weather in Texas. A sick child might use a home computer to get his schoolwork or to send a message to his teacher. Computers can make a big difference in people's lives!

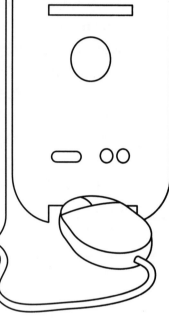

1. **Think** about the passage. **List** one way that computers are useful in **schools**.

_____

2. **Look** at the underlined words in the passage. **Circle** the letter for the answer below that best tells what the words mean.

   a. study with   b. give messages to   c. compare to

3. Why do you think the author says that computers have come a long way? **Circle** the letter for the best answer below.

   a. Computers can show places such as Alaska and Texas.
   b. Computers can be sent all over the world.
   c. Computers have changed a lot over the years.

Do you agree with the last sentence of the passage? Why or why not? Write your answer on the back of this sheet.

Brain Builder

What jobs might a woman do?

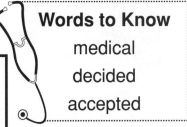

Dr. Elizabeth Blackwell

Elizabeth Blackwell grew up in the 1800s. When she was an adult, she decided that she wanted to be a doctor. There was one problem, though. Medical schools had never before accepted female students! Elizabeth looked for a long time before she found a school that would let her attend.

The idea of a woman in medical school was new to people. A lot of people thought Elizabeth was strange to study medicine. They did not treat her kindly. That did not stop Elizabeth, though. She became the first woman in the United States to finish medical school.

Later Elizabeth opened a hospital. People began to see how important her work was. <u>A lot of women followed Elizabeth's path</u>. Now there are many female doctors!

1. **Read** the words below. For each one, **write** the letter for its meaning.

   ____ decide   a. complete
   ____ finish   b. go to
   ____ attend   c. approve
   ____ accept   d. choose

2. **Look** at the underlined sentence in the passage. **Circle** the letter below for the answer that best shows what it means.

   a. Other women went on Elizabeth's street.
   b. Many women went to medical school just as Elizabeth had.
   c. Elizabeth and many other women went on a trip.

3. Do you think it is easier or harder for a woman to become a doctor today than in the 1800s? Why? _____

   _____

Brain Builder

Think about the passage. On the back of this sheet, write two words that describe Elizabeth Blackwell. Write why you chose the words.

What do you know about space travel?

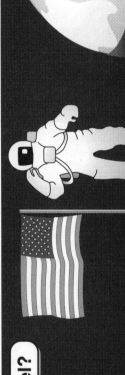

Words to Know

mankind

astronaut

spacecraft

"That's one small step for a man, one giant leap for mankind." Neil Armstrong said these words on July 20, 1969, when he first stepped on the moon.

Armstrong had worked hard to be the first man on the moon. He and two other astronauts trained for more than a year. Finally, they launched a spacecraft named *Apollo 11.* They flew it toward the moon. Then Armstrong and astronaut Edwin Aldrin used a smaller spacecraft to land on the moon. They walked on the moon and took pictures. They picked up rocks and soil to study. They also put a United States flag on the moon.

The men were heroes when they came back to Earth. Now Neil Armstrong's first step on the moon is part of history!

1. **Underline** the sentence in the passage that tells when Neil Armstrong walked on the moon.

2. **Number** the sentences below in the correct order.
   a. _____ The astronauts gathered moon rocks.
   b. _____ The astronauts returned to Earth as heroes.
   c. _____ Armstrong said, "That's one small step for a man, one giant leap for mankind."
   d. _____ Armstrong and the other astronauts trained to go to the moon.

3. **Read** the titles below. **Circle** the best one for the passage.
   a. Moon Rocks
   b. The First Moon Landing
   c. The Solar System

4. How did you decide on your answer for number 3?

   _____

   _____

Brain Builder

Look back at the first sentence in the passage. On the back of this sheet, explain what it means to you.

©2001 The Education Center, Inc. • *Comprehension Connections* • TEC4111 • Key p. 64

FAMOUS FIRSTS: *Moon landing*

What does it mean to be equal?

Thurgood Marshall

In the early 1900s, Black Americans could not go to the same schools as white people. They could not use the same waiting rooms or water fountains. Thurgood Marshall wanted to change that. He thought people should be treated the same.

Thurgood was a lawyer. <u>He argued many cases to help make sure that people were treated fairly.</u> In one case, he won the right for black students to go to the same schools as white students.

Later, the president of the United States asked Thurgood to be a Supreme Court justice. Thurgood took the job, becoming the first Black American to serve on the highest U.S. court. Thurgood continued to stand up for equal rights. He was a Supreme Court justice for 24 years.

Words to Know

justice

Supreme Court

rights

1. **Look** at the underlined sentence in the passage. **Circle** the letter for the answer below that tells what *cases* means.

   a. lawsuits   b. boxes   c. small letters

2. How were Black Americans treated in the early 1900s? **Explain.**

   _____

   _____

3. Why do you think there were no Black American Supreme Court justices before Thurgood Marshall? _____

   _____

Brain Builder

What traits do you think Supreme Court justices should have? Why? Write your ideas on the back of this sheet.

Round Up the Details!

Read the passage. **Write** the topic in the center circle below and then **choose** six words related to it. **Write** each word in a different section. **List** related details in the space that is left.

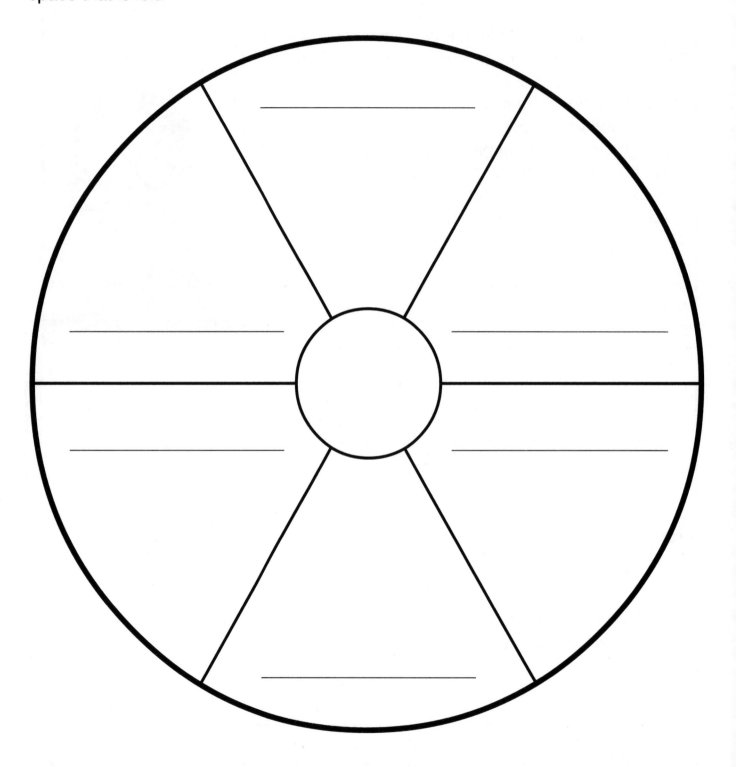

Note to the teacher: Give each student a copy of this sheet. After he completes the sheet as directed, assign students to small groups. Ask each student to read his word choices to his group members and to explain why he selected the words. Then invite a representative from each group to tell the class about the similarities and differences among the group members' word choices.

Name _____

Hot on the Trail!

Read the passage to uncover facts about _____.
Follow your teacher's directions to take notes.

Questions or Thoughts
I Have

_____
_____
_____
_____
_____
_____
_____
_____

Facts I Learned
by Reading

_____
_____
_____
_____
_____
_____
_____
_____

Facts I Already Know

_____
_____
_____
_____
_____
_____
_____
_____

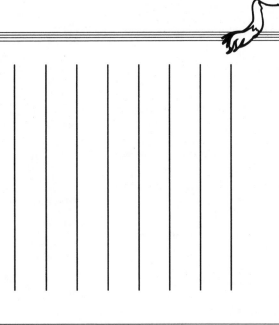

Note to the teacher: Make one copy of this page. Program the blank with the topic of a chosen passage. Then give each student one copy. On the first pictured notebook, the youngster lists facts she already knows about the topic. The student reads the passage. Then she writes information she learned from it on the second notebook. On the third notebook, she writes any questions she has about the topic or thoughts she has in response to the passage. Encourage students to share their thoughts with the class and to determine ways to find answers for their questions, such as rereading the passage or exploring other provided resources.

Answer Keys

Page 6
1. breathe, reproduce, and grow
2. offspring
3. Energy from food helps living things grow.
4. Possible answers include the following: They are alike because they are both living things. They both breathe. They are different because fish breathe through gills, but plants breathe through their leaves.
Brain Builder: Answers will vary. Accept any reasonable responses.

Page 7
1. b, a, c
2. a. F, b. O, c. O
3. Their source of food is decreasing. It is difficult for them to get enough food to survive.
Brain Builder: Answers will vary. Accept any reasonable responses.

Page 8
1. a. P, b. C, c. C, d. P, e. C, f. P
2. Without the sun, the grass would not be able to pass energy to the cows.
3. Answers will vary. Accept any reasonable responses.
Brain Builder: Answers will vary. Accept any reasonable responses.

Page 9
1. observe
2. How it looks and grows will give clues about how healthy it is.
3. a. turn yellow
   b. grow well and be healthy
   c. wilt
Brain Builder: Answers will vary. Accept any reasonable responses.

Page 10
1. a. unique   c. anchor
   b. survive   d. shallow
2. a. O, b. F, c. F
3. Answers will vary. Accept any reasonable responses.
Brain Builder: Answers will vary. Accept any reasonable responses.

Page 11
1. dandelions
2. b
3. Accept any three of the following: Seeds stick to animals' fur. Seeds are dropped by animals. Seeds are blown by the wind. Seeds float on water to new places.
Brain Builder: Answers will vary. Accept any reasonable responses.

Page 12
1. Different types of teeth help mammals eat different foods.
2. 2
3. P: giraffe, cow, deer; M: wolf, tiger, bobcat
4. Animals use teeth as tools to cut, tear, and grind food. They are important because they help the animals get and eat the food they need to survive.
Brain Builder: Answers will vary. Accept any reasonable responses.

Page 13
1. b, a, d, c
2. Accept any two of the following: good balance, long arms, the shape of their fingers, and sharp claws.
3. Koalas depend on eucalyptus trees for food. They also use them for their homes.
Brain Builder: Koalas live in Australia because that is the main place that they can get the food they need.

Page 14
1. nurse, warm-blooded, hair
2. They rest during the day and come out at night.
3. a. T, b. F, c. F, d. T
4. Answers will vary but should include that bats can quickly maneuver to change direction as they fly.
Brain Builder: Bats are like all other mammals because they are warm-blooded, have hair, and nurse their young. They are different from some mammals because they are nocturnal. They are the only mammals that fly.

Page 15
1. Accept any three of the following traits: All birds are vertebrates, have feathers, have beaks, and hatch from eggs.
2. a. (vertebrates)
   b. [continent]
3. Eggs that are laid in sheltered places do not need protective coloring because they are hidden from predators. Coloring helps camouflage eggs that are laid in open places.
4. Birds are amazing animals!
Brain Builder: Answers will vary. Accept any reasonable responses.

Page 16
1.

Bird	Diet	Beak
stork	fish	long and sharp
vulture	meat	hooked
finch	seeds	shaped like a cone
warbler	insects	short and thin

2. Answers will vary but should include that a bird's beak gives a hint about the type of food it eats.
Brain Builder: Drawings and answers will vary. Accept any reasonable responses.

Page 17
1. b
2. Each bird builds a nest that is right for its environment and for raising its young.
3. Answers will vary. Accept any reasonable responses.
4. Answers will vary but should include that birds use the materials that are available in their environments to build nests.
Brain Builder: Answers will vary. Accept any reasonable responses.

Page 18
Fish
I. How fish are different
  A. Colors
    1. camouflage
    2. warn enemies about their poison
  B. Shapes
    1. Rays and flounder are flat.
    2. Tuna look like torpedoes.
  C. Sizes
    1. less than an inch long
    2. more than 40 feet long
  D. Traits
    1. Puffers can blow up their bodies like balloons.
    2. Electric eels can make electricity.

II. How fish are alike
  A. They have backbones.
  B. They breathe mainly with gills.
  C. Most have fins.
  D. Most are cold-blooded.
  E. They live mainly in the water.

Brain Builder: Answers will vary. Accept any reasonable responses.

Page 19
1. Some fish eat plants.
2. Accept any one of the following reasons: Fish are a big source of food. Fish help keep the earth healthy. Fish help people determine whether the earth is healthy.
3. Fish help the earth stay healthy by keeping the number of plants and animals in balance.
4. Fish are hurt by water pollution. Most of the earth is water, so scientists can learn about the health of the earth by studying the health of fish.
Brain Builder: Answers will vary. Accept any reasonable responses.

Page 20
1. hearing, smell, sight
2. see
3. The passage tells about a shark's super senses. They make the shark a sensational, or amazing, animal.
4. fish, hunters, unique
Brain Builder: Answers will vary. Accept any reasonable responses.

Page 21
1. A glacier might move only 12 inches a day.
2. a. grind   c. melt
   b. weight   d. ridges
3. Possible answers include the following: It cuts through mountains and makes valleys. It might create a new lake or river. It moves rocks and soil. It might leave ridges or hills.
Brain Builder: Answers will vary. Accept any reasonable responses.

Page 22
1. 3, 1, 2
2. c, b, d, a
3. They can improve their ability to predict earthquakes, giving people more time to prepare for them and take necessary precautions.
Brain Builder: Answers will vary. Accept any reasonable responses.

Page 23
1. vent
2. lava
3. Ashes from volcanoes are good for soil, and they help plants grow.
4. Answers will vary. Accept any reasonable responses.
5. Answers will vary. Accept any reasonable responses.
Brain Builder: Answers will vary. Accept any reasonable responses.

Page 24
1. star, hot, gas, useful
2. burning gases
3. Accept any three of the following reasons: The sun gives off light and energy. It keeps the earth warm. It helps plants and animals grow. The energy from the sun can be used to heat water and homes. All life depends on the sun.
4. Answers will vary. Accept any reasonable responses.
Brain Builder: Answers will vary. Accept any reasonable responses.

Page 25
1. The order of answers may vary. Accept any reasonable responses. (Examples follow.)
   a. Earth is the only planet that has enough oxygen for people.
   b. Most of Earth is covered by water.
   c. Earth is a good distance from the sun for living things.
2. c
3. Earth
Brain Builder: Answers will vary. Accept any reasonable responses.

Page 26
1. They are small, solid planets made of rock and metal.
2. It has frozen water at its poles like Earth does.
3.

Planet	Order From the Sun	Temperature	Atmosphere	Other Information
Earth	third	mild	people can breathe	has living things
Mars	fourth	cold	thin, people can't breathe	covered with red dust
Mercury	first	very hot	almost none	has a lot of craters
Venus	second	hotter than Mercury	thick and poisonous	has a lot of clouds

Brain Builder: Answers will vary. Accept any reasonable responses.

Page 27
1. They take up space and have weight.
2. juice, gravy, notebook, river
3. A solid has a definite shape, but a liquid does not.
Brain Builder: Answers will vary. Accept any reasonable responses.

Page 28
1. a. measure
   b. definite
   c. unique
   d. describe
   e. space
2. a. T, b. T, c. F
3. A bowl of cake batter has a greater mass than a feather because it has more matter.
Brain Builder: Answers will vary. Accept any reasonable responses.

Page 29
1. Answers will vary. Accept any reasonable responses.
2. Accept any of the following: gas, electricity, or fire.
3. wood, plastic
4. a. because it is a poor heat conductor.
   b. it is called conduction.
   c. because it is a good heat conductor.
Brain Builder: Answers will vary. Accept any reasonable responses.

Page 30
1. Accept any two of the following: to turn on lights, heat homes, make cars go, enable people and animals to move, or help people and animals grow.
2. a. sound   c. sun
   b. water   d. energy
3. Answers will vary. Accept any reasonable responses.
Brain Builder: Answers will vary. Accept any reasonable responses.

Page 31
1. a. escapes
   b. absorb
   c. transfers
   d. pale
2. a. E, C
   b. C, E
   c. C, E
Brain Builder: The person should wear dark clothes because dark colors absorb heat.

Page 32
1. b
2. a. F, b. T, c. F
3. The shadow would become larger.
4. Shadows are not just fun to observe; they are helpful, too.
Brain Builder: You would probably not see shadows because the clouds would block some or all of the sun, and light is needed to make shadows.

Page 33
1. c
2. c, b, a
3. The Native Americans built their homes with the materials available in their regions.
Brain Builder: Answers will vary. Accept any reasonable responses.

Page 34
1. a. Japan
   b. China
   c. Mexico
   d. Russia
2. Regions and customs affect what people eat and how their food is served.
3. People in China use chopsticks to eat, and people in the United States use forks.
Brain Builder: Answers will vary but should include foods that are red and white because people in Japan eat red and white foods on New Year's Day for good luck.

Page 35
1. b, d, a, c, e
2. hurling
3. The players try to break the piñata open.
Brain Builder: Answers will vary. Accept any reasonable responses.

Page 36
1. c
2. d, a, c, b
3. Answers will vary. Accept any reasonable responses.
Brain Builder: Answers will vary. Accept any reasonable responses.

Page 37
1. disk
2. a. hourglass
   b. burning
   c. exact
   d. shadow
3. Possible answers include the following: It must be a sunny day to use a sundial. Sundials are not very accurate. They are not convenient to carry.
Brain Builder: Answers will vary. Accept any reasonable responses.

Page 38
1. b
2. 1, 3, 2
3. Answers will vary. Accept any reasonable responses.
Brain Builder: Answers will vary. Accept any reasonable responses.

Page 39
1. c, d, e, b, a
2. more than half
3. Answers will vary but should reflect that landforms are features of the earth's surface.
Brain Builder: Drawings will vary but should show an island completely surrounded by water and a peninsula that is almost surrounded by water. Writing will vary but may include that an island and a peninsula are both landforms that are at least partially bordered by water.

Page 40
1. candle, blanket, bike, books, stove
2. Trees are an important resource because they provide oxygen and shade. They are also a source for lumber and paper.
3. Answers will vary. Accept any reasonable responses.
Brain Builder: Answers will vary. Accept any reasonable responses.

Page 41
1. a. M
   b. G, M
   c. G, M
   d. G
   e. M
2. a. model
   b. entire
3. Answers will vary. Accept any reasonable responses.
Brain Builder: Answers will vary. Accept any reasonable responses.

Page 42
1. crews
2. Accept any three of the following: make clothes, fill cavities, deliver mail, make trucks, keep streets in good shape, and keep the roads safe.
3. Answers may vary. Accept responses such as the following:
   a. The roads would not be kept in as good condition. The postal workers might have difficulty traveling as they deliver the mail.
   b. There would be no trucks. The postal workers would need to find other means of transportation. They might not be able to deliver the mail as quickly.
Brain Builder: Answers will vary. Accept any reasonable responses.

Page 43
1. Answers will vary. Accept any reasonable responses.
2. Bananas do not grow well in the United States. Trading is the best way for people in the United States to get this fruit.
3. c
Brain Builder: Answers will vary but should include that with trade it is possible for countries to get things that they do not have or do not have in large enough supply.

Page 44
1. People bartered for things.
2. a. business
   b. value
   c. goods
   d. weaver
   e. services
3. A farmer would probably have a greater surplus of corn than wood or tools.
Brain Builder: Answers will vary. Accept any reasonable responses.

Page 45
1. c
2. a. casts
   b. election
   c. citizens
   d. candidate
3. An election is a voting process used to make a choice.
Brain Builder: Answers will vary. Accept any reasonable responses.

Page 46
1. a. local
   b. state
   c. national
2. a. in the state capitol
   b. in city hall
3. The governor would be the best person to tell because he is the leader at the state level.
Brain Builder: Answers will vary. Accept any reasonable responses.

Page 47
1. c, d, a, b
2. Accept any two of the following duties: The president works with the leaders of other countries, is the commander in chief of the armed forces, helps make sure people obey the national laws, works with people to get new laws approved, goes to ceremonies and celebrations, and sometimes throws the first ball of the baseball season.
3. a. O, b. F, c. O
Brain Builder: Answers will vary. Accept any reasonable responses.

Page 48
1. 4, 1, 2, 3
2. He saw the American flag still flying over the fort.
3. He was proud of his country and wanted to celebrate the victory.
Brain Builder: Answers will vary. Accept any reasonable responses.

Page 49
1. d, c, a, b
2. Accept any of the following: They close schools, hold parades, put flags and flowers on soldiers' graves, and float small ships filled with flowers in the harbors.
3. a. F, b. F, c. O, d. O
Brain Builder: Answers will vary. Accept any reasonable responses.

Page 50
1. immigrant
2. a. New York Harbor
   b. doctors
3. They were poor and unhappy in their countries. They wanted to start new, free lives in America.
4. Now there is a museum on Ellis Island.
Brain Builder: Answers will vary. Accept any reasonable responses.

Page 51
1. When he was a very young child, Mozart could play and write music well.
2. harpsichord
3. b
4. musical, composer, gifted
Brain Builder: Responses will vary. Accept any reasonable responses.

Page 52
1. Accept any of the following responses: Sacagawea communicated with the Shoshone people, she helped get horses for the explorers, she helped the Shoshone people understand that the explorers were friendly, and she helped get food for the explorers.
2. b
3. journey
4. a. F, b. F, c. O, d. O
Brain Builder: Answers will vary. Accept any reasonable responses.

Page 53
1. 3, 4, 2, 1
2. a. F, b. T, c. F
3. Answers will vary. Accept any reasonable responses.
Brain Builder: Answers will vary. Accept any reasonable responses.

Page 54
1. Accept any reasonable responses similar to the following: A plow loosens soil and makes it easier to plant seeds. Plowing also adds air to the soil, enhancing plant growth.
2. Plants grow faster in plowed soil because the soil has more air.
3. a. F, b. O, c. F
4. Answers will vary. Accept any reasonable responses.
Brain Builder: Responses will vary but should include any two of the following reasons: A plow loosens the soil, making it easier to plant seeds. Plowing helps plants grow better. A plow is a machine that makes a farmer's work easier by doing work that the farmer would otherwise do by hand.

Page 55
1. b, e, a, d, c
2. Answers will vary. Accept any reasonable responses.
3. Cameras are less expensive. They are also easier and faster to use.
Brain Builder: Answers will vary. Accept any reasonable responses.

Page 56
1. Accept any of the following responses: Students can learn from computers. They can play games on computers. They can use computers to communicate with people all around the world. They can use computers to check the weather in other parts of the world. They can use home computers to communicate with teachers at school.
2. b
3. c
Brain Builder: Answers will vary. Accept any reasonable responses.

Page 57
1. d, a, b, c
2. b
3. Answers will vary. Accept any reasonable responses.
Brain Builder: Answers will vary. Accept any reasonable responses.

Page 58
1. Neil Armstrong said these words on July 20, 1969, when he first stepped on the moon.
2. a. 3, b. 4, c. 2, d. 1
3. b
4. Answers will vary. Accept any reasonable responses.
Brain Builder: Answers will vary. Accept any reasonable responses.

Page 59
1. a
2. Answers will vary but should include that Black Americans were discriminated against and were segregated from white people.
3. Answers will vary. Accept any reasonable responses.
Brain Builder: Answers will vary. Accept any reasonable responses.